I0786891

Substitute Teaching in the 2020s:
A Simple Guide

Julien Morizio

| RESPONSIVE TUTORING

Available for all students, from anywhere, anytime

Dedication

To the individuals in communities who have a shortage of teachers and choose to support their local school and its students the best they can. Your service and presence in the school provide such relief for the staff and ensures that the students are taken care of. I wish you the best of luck and hope that this book serves you well.

To the individuals who wish to have a career as a substitute teacher. This job can be challenging, yet rewarding. Although you might not necessarily follow your students' academic careers for more than one day at a time, your presence means a lot to them and you can make a difference in their lives with every interaction. You will surely develop methods and approaches of your own based on your experiences. Hopefully this book offers you a chance to ease into the profession, or give you ideas so that the rewards outweigh the challenges.

To the future educators who are at the early stages of their profession, every opportunity to teach and to be in the presence of students is an opportunity to learn and perfect your craft. This book is there to provide you with simple reminders and guidelines to help you early on as you get acquainted with different students from different classes from different schools. Hang in there and remember to always use what works best for you. The better you are in the classroom, the greater impact you will have on students' lives.

Table of Contents

Introduction

If you have picked up this book, you have probably noticed the endless supply of resources on the topic of substitute teaching. If you are looking for a complete guide with detailed instructions, activities, and bonus templates, this book is not it. As the title indicates, this book is a simple guide. If you want to be the best substitute teacher you can be, hours spent in the classroom would benefit you a lot more, and your students, than time spent with a book. Substitute teaching, just like teaching, is something you get better at with practice and experience. Of course, some preliminary knowledge can help you perform well early on. However, that knowledge is not exhaustive. I promise you, all you need to know is contained in this little book. Its purpose is to provide you with a good foundation. You will surely develop your subbing acumen on your own as you see what works best for you. After all, we are all different. Just like one learning style does not match all students, teaching styles are unique to every educator.

This guide was written with the high school environment in mind as high school students tend to be more inclined to give their substitute teachers a hard time. However, the concepts discussed in this book do not change for elementary students. Younger students tend to be more compliant. What they mostly need is a little more attention and consolation from the adult in the room. Adopt a more warm and comforting approach than you would with teenagers, and they will appreciate you. Students from Kindergarten to Grade 2 might even ask for a hug by the end of your time with them.

To get the most out of this book, remember the three most important principles to keep in mind to sub effectively:

- Structure
- Empathy
- Fairness

As long as you try your best to understand the kids and give them structure, they will perceive you as being fair and will be on board with you to have a good class. If they do not find you fair, then they will let you know in the way they behave.

The best mindset when subbing is really to have the students and yourself on the same side. You both want to have a good class. The students want to succeed. You, assumedly, want to do a good job. These goals are not mutually exclusive. The only thing that must be kept at bay is the group's tendency to want to rebel. But that is simple, a little give-and-take can prevent that, as you will see in this book.

Furthermore, every recommendation or strategy shared in this book has been tried by myself in the field. If they did not work for me, then I would not have included them in this book. I have only included strategies that have worked on multiple occasions for myself. Nonetheless, since we are working with individuals, and situations change from one to the next, keep in mind that these recommendations are not set in stone. Whenever possible, they should be modified to best fit the situation you find yourself in.

Before Going to the School

You might receive the call or email from the secretary, the principal, the teacher who needs a replacement, or someone working at the school board who is in charge of finding substitute teachers. If you wish to be on their good list, say "yes" to subbing jobs as much as possible. The more you make yourself available for them, the more they will prioritize you the next time they need a sub. That is of course if you do a good job.

Now, you have agreed to sub and have taken note of the name of the school and its address. Before you go to the school, make sure you find out what kind of school it is. Visit the school's website and familiarize yourself with its mission statement. It will give you an idea of what is expected of its teachers. For example, if it is a school that is specialized in teaching children with severe learning disabilities, it would be good to know so in advance so that you can prepare to give its students the attention they need. Or, it could be a school that puts a strong emphasis on student-centered learning, in which case the students are more autonomous, and you would not have to come in as strict. Oftentimes, if the school that calls you is public and has a general mission statement, then you could expect to follow the guidelines in this book more closely.

While you are on the website, take note of the principal and vice-principal's name in case you run into them. If available, familiarize yourself with the daily schedule. You might also want to take note of the school's phone number just in case of an emergency.

Most often, especially for public schools, you will only get to know the instructions from the teacher you are replacing once the secretary gives them to you in a sub folder or you see them awaiting you on the teacher's desk. There are some cases, mostly with private or independent schools, when you are emailed the instructions in advance. If that is the case, then familiarize yourself with them so that you know what to expect and also if you have to get any out-of-class materials beforehand.

In case you wonder what material to bring to the school, at the very least bring a pen. Also, it is always a good idea to bring post-it notes and maybe even some loose leaf. They can come in handy.

When commuting, plan to make it to the school about half an hour before the period you sub for to give yourself ample time. Showing up late is not an option. In case there is traffic, you will still be on time. Also, there are sometimes some last-minute things to do to set up the class. For example, the teacher might leave a DVD for you to play for the students. If there is no DVD player or laptop in the class, then you will have enough time to find someone who can help you. If you wait until the very last minute, it will be hard to find someone who is willing to help, and besides, you might be busy letting students into the classroom at that point. The last image you want to project of yourself is one of panic. The more time you give yourself, the more chance you have of coming across as someone who is in control. That is the image that commands respect from the students.

Before the Bell

It is now ten minutes before class starts. Either you are in the hallway, waiting for the class that was in before you to wrap up, or are already in the classroom. Regardless, there are a few things you should do. As soon as you have the chance to be in the classroom, familiarize yourself with the environment and find where the teacher keeps their chalk or marker to write on the blackboard or whiteboard. Write your name and the date. Afterwards, write down "Task" and then list what the teacher has written for the students to do. On the following page, you will see an example of what your board would look like:

Tuesday, February 4th, 2020

Mr. Morizio

Task: - Read Ch. 8-9 of "To Kill a Mockingbird"

- Complete questions on Ch. 8-9

- Hand them in to me

- Work on individual projects

That is all you need to write. It might look simple, but just doing that prevents a lot of fuss. When the students walk in, they know exactly what they will be doing. None will have to ask. When it comes time to share the task with them, it would only serve as a confirmation rather than an announcement. No student will be confused about their task for that period. They will also know how to address you. Furthermore, they will never need to ask what the day's date is, which otherwise could cause many unnecessary interruptions.

Notice the "Hand them in to me" detail. While that statement might not directly be part of the task, it clarifies what the students are expected to do for the period. With that detail mentioned, students will be less likely to ask, "Is it for homework?" or "What do we do when we are finished?" Additional details are therefore good to mention only if they serve to clarify while still keeping the overall task simple. The whole purpose is to provide students with structure from the outset. The more students know what is expected of them, the less the odds are that they will cause interruptions and prevent the period from having a good flow.

The Best Approach

The preliminary setup is done. Now, either you are waiting for the students to come into the classroom, or some have already trickled in with you while you were getting ready. It is important at this point to keep in mind how you come across to the students. Remember, you want to come across as someone in control. If you are in control, then students can expect you to be fair and provide them with structure. Panic and nervousness do not give off the same impression. If you tend to be a nervous or shy person, you can still give the impression that you are in control. Just make sure you have taken care of everything that has been discussed, namely the preliminary setup. If you know the tasks that the teacher has left for the students and have made them visible to the students by writing them on the board, then you are in control. The most essential part is done. All you have to do now is wait for the class to officially begin.

Make sure to sit at or stay near the teacher's desk. Sometimes, a student will test you by sitting on the teacher's chair. Sitting at the teacher's desk automatically limits that confrontation from becoming possible. It also establishes you as the teacher's replacement for the day.

While waiting for the bell, you might wonder how to be. Do you behave as you normally would, showing the students your personality? You might be tempted to think that the students, seeing a substitute, will automatically be reasonable, be on your side, and make things easy for you since you are not their actual teacher. You might also think that they will respect you more if you just act like yourself. You can try, but that is rarely the case. While there is no need to be uptight and ruthlessly strict, there is a fine balance that goes into the approach that elicits the best response from students.

To understand this approach, you must understand the difference between a friendly teacher, and a "laid back" yet fair teacher. Mentally, you can make that distinction in your mind by asking yourself this: Outside of school, would it be okay to hang out with these students? Unless you live in a small town where everybody is friends with each other or remotely related, the answer is definitely no. You are the adult in the room and adults are not usually friends with teenagers. Just because you are not friendly per se, does not mean you have to be mean. The calm, collected, fair teacher is the one that children appreciate. In their words, that is the kind of teacher who is "chill."

As the students enter the classroom, and they pass by your immediate field of vision, you can greet them as it might otherwise be rude. A courteous "Hello" would do, but do not actively try to seek a response or build a rapport with the students at the beginning of class. The students do not see you as their teacher. They see you as an adult. Trying to build a rapport would be similar to trying to befriend, and that can contradict the image of yourself as the adult in the room.

This may seem unreasonable but personally, unless I know the students, I try not to make any eye contact with them before the bell. I either keep busy with the forms and attendance sheets in front of me, as not to look disrespectful, or look around the classroom to acclimatize myself. If I unintentionally make eye contact with a student or if they say "Hi", then I say it back. Otherwise, they are busy talking to friends about what happened last night, or at recess, or during last class. By not engaging with them as soon as they step inside the classroom, you give them a chance to settle in and finish their break between periods. You are already on their side by not intruding. You understand the dynamic, and they respect that from you right away. When the bell then rings, they are eager to hear you as you greet them all together.

Getting Their Attention

The bell for the period rings. The students are wrapping up their conversations among friends. Sometimes the bell is not enough to signal the beginning of class. It is up to you to signal this transition. You can simply do so by making an adjustment to your position. While the students might appear busy doing something else, they are all, at varying degrees, paying attention to what you are doing. By physically responding to the bell, you are implying a shift from whatever came before class and what is coming next. If you were sitting down at the teacher's desk, stand up. If you were already standing, go to the door and have a final look in the hallway to see if there are any students running late or congregating by the door. Come back and leave the door open. Why leave the door open? It shows the students that you expect them to be quiet. A substitute teacher, fearing that the class will get loud, might close the door from the get-go to prevent disturbing other classes near yours. Remember, the image you want to project is that of being in control and of having high expectations.

When you return to the desk, look at the entire class and greet them. You can say something as simple as "Hello everyone." There is no need to shout to get their attention. If you shout from the very beginning, that does not portray someone who is in control, and students would likely not respond favorably. If some students are still not at their places, calmly say, "Let's get seated." At this point, many students if not most are already looking at you to start the class. If others are still talking, they will most likely be advised by their classmates that you, the sub, are trying to talk and that class has begun. If needed, repeat the greeting one final time when there is silence and all students are seated.

I follow my greeting with "How are you?" Some substitute teachers tend to avoid starting with a question, again because they fear opening up the floodgates. They might think that you are inviting the whole class to talk. In fact, you are doing so, but that is not necessarily a bad thing. Sometimes there are students who need to share something. Something might have happened during recess or the previous class and they are antsy to get it off their chest. Instead of having them go against the rules you will set, invite them to get it off their chest at the beginning. Say something like this:

"Your teacher left some work for you to do. While you do it, there will need to be silence so that you can all focus. I understand though if there are some things you need to tell each other first, so if that is the case, raise your hand to share it with the class."

If their concerns are not a big deal, they will save it for later to communicate it one-on-one with a classmate. If they are a big deal and they involve many in the room, then they might say something. Invite students to speak one at a time, and do not allow others to interrupt. When the major details come out, turn it into a teachable moment as best as you can. Refer to the universal truths of being kind to each other, respecting each other's differences, and focusing on yourself. Finish off with connecting to why it is important to do your best today and that it involves doing well in school. That segues smoothly into the work the teacher left for them to do.

Chances are the class will not actually begin this way. It has happened to me though that I sensed the students were jittery about something and that it would be hopeless to expect them to work in silence from the beginning. So this strategy of asking how they were and giving them a chance to speak served me and the class well every time I used it. I only did so when I found it necessary. Oftentimes though, asking them how they are is just a sign of courtesy. You might get some single-word responses like "good," after which you can tell them the tasks their teacher has left for them to do.

Cover Your Bases

You greeted the class, you introduced yourself, you told them the task for the day, and you took their questions if they had any. You did your job, but it is not over yet. Depending on the school, you might have another 45 minutes or more than an hour left with them. A lot can transpire within that time. That is why the first minutes are very crucial; they set the tone for the entire period. One thing you should do, after sharing the teacher's instructions, is cover your bases.

When students finish their work, they are left unstructured. As a result, some start talking to people beside them, get up to talk to friends further away, congregate in a corner, sit on the window ledge, create games with class materials, etc. Obviously, you would like to avoid the potential for chaos. So how do you prevent that from happening? Create structure for after they complete their work. Here is where students can help you. Once you get used to subbing, you can offer options that you know the students will appreciate. Before then, ask them to come up with their own options. The conversation goes something like this:

"Now I know that some of you are quick and will finish this work before class ends. So, what are a couple of things you can do after you finish that won't disturb others?"

Here is a list of potential answers from the students:

- Reading a book they brought with them or from the class library
- Doodle or write
- Do homework from another class
- Listen to music
- Take a nap at their desk
- If there is an ongoing project that they are working on, then they might mention that

Once you discuss the options that you feel are appropriate, it is always best to remind them that as long as they remain silent and seated, then it is allowed. The purpose is to have them hear the options and know your expectations. That way, there is no chance that they will roam around aimlessly once they finish their work.

Give and Take

Here is where you get crafty, but still keep it simple. These are young kids you are dealing with. Yes, they want to do well in school, but they also want to have fun. The fact that they are surrounded by their friends only encourages the latter tendency. Here is where you can cut a deal with them. But be careful! You might get tempted to say something like this:

"If you behave well and finish your work, then I will let you have free time."

There is very little structure in such a statement. It leaves students with plenty of opportunities to ask questions:

"Are we good enough yet?"

"We worked for 15 minutes, is that enough?"

Soon after they start asking these questions to which you cannot provide a fair answer, they will turn against you and begin having free time on their own terms.

Time is very good for structure. Allocate a certain amount of time for the work and reward. I like the model of 40-40-20, which I call the 3-phase system:

- Phase 1: 40% individual work in silence
- Phase 2: 40% listen to music or work quietly with a student beside you
- Phase 3: 20% structured free time

If the class is 75 minutes long, that means that the first two phases should be 30 minutes long, with the final one being 15 minutes (or the time remaining). If the class is an hour long, assign 25 minutes to the first two phases, and 10 to the last. If the class is 50 minutes long, I recommend assigning 20 minutes to the first two phases, with the last taking the remainder of the period. The 40-40-20 model is a framework that you can adjust as you best see fit. I would avoid assigning overly specific time lengths like 22 minutes though, as students might deem that to be weird and question your fairness or judgment. Numbers that end in 0 or 5 just sound more right.

This format works. Why? It sets the tone from the start: one of quiet work. When you will allow the students to work with partners, the tone will persist since it has already been set. If you were to allow them to work with friends from the start, they might talk about anything else but their work. It would then be hard for them to ever get to their actual work. You avoid that from happening by having the students work from the beginning, and they will do so for two reasons: they want to do well, they want to earn your permission to work with a partner.

Be strict in enforcing these timelines. If you ask for 30 minutes of silent work, do not begin your "timer" until there is absolute silence. I put timer in brackets because, while you can use your watch (or cell phone), simply referring to the clock in the classroom would do. Let them know when you begin the timer. Restart it if you hear a student speak without having raised their hand. Let them know when/if you restart the timer. Five minutes before the next step, let them know about the time and the good work they have been doing. Positive reinforcement is effective, as long as you use it sparingly.

Maintaining Students' Focus

Once you have provided the students with what they need to know to begin working, circulate around the classroom to make sure they are all doing what they should be doing. If their task is to work on pages in their textbook, make sure they have their book open. If they are asked to work on a project on their laptops, make sure they have the right file or tab open on their screen. If they are working on a handout you just distributed, make sure they all have it and are working on it.

Circulate is not to be mistaken with policing. Yes, you are making sure everything is orderly and that the students are on task, but you are not investigating ever single student, trying to make an arrest. The students will turn against you quickly if they sense that. Just walk at a steady yet relaxed pace in the isles between the students' desks, while glancing at the top of each student's desk – not the students themselves. They do not know you and some can get uncomfortable if you are too close to them.

Maintain a healthy distance of at least one meter from each student as you circulate.

Phase1:

While circulating, if you notice that a student has not yet begun their work, politely in a low voice, ask them if they have all they need to do their work. If they have it, then they will nod and get to their work. If the material they need is in their locker, then you can write them a note to go get it (explained in more detail in the section, "Bathroom and Leaving the Classroom"). If they do not have any access to their material (e.g. they left it at home or lost it), then ask the student sitting beside him or her if they would be willing to share the necessary material.

Once you have completed your first round of circulation and every student has officially started working, you are on standby in case they have any questions. I would not recommend standing in the front somewhere, looking at them. That might be off-putting to some. That might even prompt them to start whispering to each other about how awkward it is to have this person staring at them. Instead, I recommend to sit at the teacher's desk and act busy. If you have any paperwork to do and you brought it with you, you can go ahead and do it while intermittently just looking up to face the students. If you brought your laptop and you have work to do on it, then you can open it and leave it on the desk at an angle where the laptop does not completely block you from the students. When you act busy, you are inadvertently modeling how the students should behave as they do their work.

By working on something yourself, you are once again on their side. You, along with the students, are all busy working. It is as if you are the leader making sure that all continue to be productive. If you are at the teacher's desk, looking at your phone or just supervising them, then you might come across as the prison warden, and the students will not appreciate that. So, bring some work with you or at least a pen and paper to do some writing. You can end up being productive on your own, while also doing your job effectively as a substitute teacher.

During the first phase, circulate every 5 to 10 minutes or so.

When there are around 5 minutes left in phase 1, without shouting, advise the students and let them know that they have been working well.

Phase 2:

Mark the change in phases by saying something like this:

"Alright, you have all been working well and in silence for ______________ (time you had agreed upon). Now, you can _________________ [what you had agreed upon (listen to music or work with a partner)] if you like."

Set the new expectations for how they should conduct themselves. If you allow them to listen to music, tell them that the volume should be low enough so that no one else can hear it. If they can work with a partner, then tell them that they have to whisper. See the section on "Working in Groups" for more effective recommendations.

The students might get a little more excited since they are listening to music or working together, so make sure to circulate every 5 minutes. The tone has been set from the previous phase and the transition to the second phase. There is no need to be more rigid here.

Students will also start finishing their work, at which point they will do one of the things you had agreed were appropriate at the beginning of class (e.g. read, doodle, do other homework, etc.).

There is no need to let them know when there are five minutes left, because most would have already begun their structured free time already (although individually and relatively quietly).

Phase 3:

Mark the change in phases by saying something like this:

"Alright, you have all worked well. If you have finished your work, hand it in to me if you haven't done so already and you can have your free time (e.g. play on your phone, join your friends). Make sure to keep the volume down, though, since there are still people finishing up their work."

At this point, most would have already finished their work. If not, they might choose to take a break and complete it for homework. One thing they will not do is have a free-for-all.

Some might worry that the students are like a bottle of pop. While they were working, the bottle was being shaken. Switching to phase three would be like removing the cap, creating a huge mess. In reality, the class is more like a plane waiting for take-off. While the students are working, the plane is still parked, and the safety procedures are exchanged. Starting phase 3 is like setting the plane in motion; it has quite a way left to go on the runway before taking off. The students have earned a break, so why not let them have it? Without an impending break, then they might very well be like a shaking bottle of pop, and you would not be the one to decide when to remove the cap.

During phase 3, I would recommend closing the door and circulating a lot more. If it gets unreasonably loud, try to pinpoint the students who are causing the volume to rise and let them know, politely, that it is too loud (and not that they are). These students will take it upon themselves to lower their volume. Since they led others to get louder, they can lead others to bring the volume down as well. Always make sure that students remain seated. If one gets up, ten will follow. As soon as you see a student standing up, remind them that they have to sit down. If they seem hesitant, you can even place a chair close beside them. They always end by sitting back down.

I recommend keeping the door closed at the final minutes of class for two reasons: there is a chance that some students start taking off noise-wise, and since the end of class is approaching, you would want to discourage any student from leaving early.

Working in Groups

When you allow students either to work with a partner or to talk to friends, make sure they always remain seated. That is what is most important. As explained before, many will get up if you do not immediately tell the first one who stands up to sit down. You can do so politely. The default for students is sitting down. So as soon as they stand up, some attention is directed to you to see how you react. If you reinforce that they must remain seated, either with a sign you make with your facial expression or with a calm and firm voice, they will sit back down. If they wish to move somewhere else in the classroom to be closer to a certain student (of course, when they are allowed to do so) then tell them to bring their chair with them. As stated before, pull up a chair for them whenever necessary.

The reason why I am so stringent on having them sit down is because standing up leads to walking around which could lead to running in the classroom. Students like to move, but in the classroom, when they are excited that their teacher is not there, is not the time. Chaos is just out of the equation if students remain seated.

Furthermore, when you allow students to work together, let them know the volume that is acceptable. How do you do that? Your class's transition from individual work to groupwork is rooted in silence. Take the opportunity to set the target volume. When students begin to whisper to their partners, tell them something like this:

"Alright, this volume is good. Continue like this."

You have therefore provided the students with a reference that they themselves have generated. If ever they speak louder, advise them. Say something like this:

"It's getting loud. Lower the volume please."

You can also make signals of where the volume is by opening your hand with its palm facing the floor. Whenever the students get louder, bring your hand up and remind them where, by lowering the level of your hand, where the volume level should be brought down to.

If the task for the day involves groupwork from the beginning of the period, then you can simply do what is mentioned in this section from the beginning of the period instead of using the 3-phase system.

Attendance

Taking attendance can disrupt the flow of the lesson and can even take up a lot of class time. Students can grow impatient and start conversations with each other as you take them. Some students might even try to trick you, pretending to be students that are, in reality, absent. Luckily, there is a way more efficient and simple method than the good old shouting of names. You can simply delegate the job to a student in the class. More often than not, there is a student who wants to play teacher and loves taking attendance. They might even volunteer as soon as they come in through the door. Let them. Since they know their classmates, they will take attendance in silence.

I often ask for a volunteer after I establish the 3-phase system. I almost do it in a whisper and always get a volunteer. The only con for this method is that you do not get to know their names. But how well can you otherwise retain their names by going through thirty of them all at once. The names that can be important to take note of are those of the troublemakers. Since they draw a lot of attention, students are bound to call them by their name at a certain point, which then allows you to take note of them.

The school will have a system for how to report attendance. You might have a blue or yellow slip on which to write the absences that will be collected by the hall monitor. Or a student might volunteer to bring the completed list to the secretary's office. The secretary will often let you know what to do when it comes to that.

Additionally, the teacher you are replacing always appreciates it when they know which students missed the class. Therefore, make sure to include the names of students who were absent that day in the note you leave for them.

Leaving on a Good Note

During the final moments of class, try to keep the students seated until the bell rings to signal its end. Keeping students seated and relatively quiet might be a battle that is too hard to win at this point. There is only so much you can do, and it is okay if some get a little rowdier with a minute or two remaining. It is not time to get into a confrontation and to start yelling. You might sub again for them or at the school in the future and the word on you travels quickly throughout the student body. So leave a good impression on the students. When there is about one minute left of class, thank them for having worked well and remind them to finish their task for homework if they did not complete it in class. That is all.

When the bell rings, make sure all students leave in a timely manner (usually that is not an issue), make sure the windows are closed and put anything back in its place if necessary.

Make sure to say goodbye to the secretary on the way out and return him or her any materials if necessary.

Bathroom and Leaving the Classroom

Bathroom is one of those things that can become an issue if not treated properly and consistently. Once again, the school might have a system, in which case you would be informed, and you would adhere to it. There might even be a hall pass in the classroom that the students will inform you about if their teacher has their own system.

If that does not occur, then you need to create your own system. There is no need to let them know about it at the beginning of class. Just let the first student know when they ask to go to the bathroom and the rest will get the message.

Option #1 (Students have agendas):

a. Ask them for their agenda.
b. Ask them what their name is and check the agenda to see if it is in fact theirs.

c. Write down on the day's date the exact time, the classroom number or subject, and the place they intend to go to (in this case, write "bathroom")
d. Tell them they have 3 minutes.

Option #2 (Students do not have agendas):

a. Take a post-it note from the teacher's desk or one that you brought.
b. Write down the day's date, the exact time, the classroom number or subject, and the place they intend to go to (in this case, write "bathroom")
c. Tell them they have 3 minutes.

This method discourages the student from doing anything other than what they told you they would do. It also prevents them from lingering in the hallways to avoid class. Do not allow any student to leave until the other has returned. This way, they are not able to congregate outside the classroom and waste time together.

These options can also be used for other situations where the student has to leave, whether it is to go to the secretary's office or to see another teacher. Adjust the location on your note, as well as the time limit, accordingly. If the students are lying, the hall monitor or another staff member will ultimately find them and know, based on the note that they have with them, that they are not at the right place and will return them to the classroom. If it happens that they do not return, which rarely happens, write that as a remark in the note you leave for the teacher. Also include in that note if students had to leave early for a valid reason (e.g. attending soccer practice).

Cell Phones

Nowadays, many schools have a cell phone policy. Familiarize yourself with it. Try to find it on the school's website. If it is not there, then you can ask the secretary later when you see him or her. Oftentimes, you will know as soon as you walk in the classroom. The teacher might leave a note concerning cell phones in their instructions. They might ask you to tell the students to put their cell phones in a box in front of the room. There might also be a shoe rack or pocket system that students need to place their cell phones in.

I would never stress the cell phone issue too much. Cell phones can get misplaced or stolen, and you being the adult can be held responsible. My advice is to let the students have their cell phones in their possession unless it appears as though the school is making a big effort against students having their cell phones in class, or if the teacher gave you clear instructions to collect the cell phones. Besides, cell phones can come to your advantage, especially when using the 3-phase system detailed in the sections "Give and Take" and "Maintaining Students' Focus."

For classes like Art and Multimedia, it would be alright to allow students to use their cell phones for the entire period. They might need them to look at pictures for inspiration or to listen to music to get their creativity going. The 3-phase system might not even be necessary for these classes, as students would most probably be busy and focused on working away on their individual projects for the entire period.

Exceptional Circumstances

The recommendations in this book can be applied in most schools. They can also be adapted to fit the culture of different schools. For instance, if you are called to sub in a school that puts a big emphasis on student autonomy, then you might not have to circulate as much or provide such structure. Sometimes, you will just need to leave the students to their work and get out of their way. If you feel like you are doing nothing in those cases, that is fine. You would be there mainly to supervise and help students whenever they have questions.

These recommendations also work for most classrooms. There are some exceptions of course, like physical education, that might call for different approaches. No matter what, let empathy, structure, and fairness guide your approach.

As an example, there were multiple instances when I had to sub for physical education. The teacher had left no lesson for me. Once the students had changed into their gym clothes, I asked them what they did the previous class and if they would like to do it again this period. That opened the conversation, through which they decided upon what games to play for the period. I was alright with their pick as long as they did not go crazy. This approach worked for every physical education class I subbed for. Why?

- I empathised with them: I understood that they were excited to have gym class and would probably want to play games of their own choosing. So, I let them.
- I provided them with structure: We agreed upon the games they would be playing. There would therefore not be any students randomly playing with other gym equipment around the gymnasium.
- I was fair: I was okay with what they wanted to do, as long as they conducted themselves appropriately.

Use those three principles – empathy, structure, and fairness – and you will have a successful class every time.

If a Teacher Leaves Behind a Detailed Lesson Plan

As already mentioned, the instructions that the teacher leaves for you often consist of a list of work to assign to their students. Very rarely do they expect the substitute teacher to teach a lesson. They are aware that the substitute teacher might not specialize in their subject area and that it would be difficult to expect someone from outside their school to do their job just like they would.

Sometimes, though, a teacher will require the substitute teacher to teach a certain concept or to run a detailed lesson/activity. If that is the case, then there are two things you should at least do:

1. Make sure the students know the homework (most essential).
2. Do your best (all that can be expected of you).

Yes, it is important to teach a good lesson. However, it might be hard when you do not know the students or the subject material. Focus on what you are most in control of, which is letting the students know what is expected of them from their teacher. In that case, the students would at least have completed their work by the next time their teacher sees them. If the students do their work, then they are on schedule with the teacher's schedule. The teacher will re-explain certain topics if they need to. Since you will not be teaching their students for long, it is alright if your attempts at teaching them do not go perfectly. Their teacher does not expect you to perform as well as they do. But still try your best when teaching the students if you are asked to do so. Chances are they will learn a thing or two from you.

Making a Good Impression on the Teacher

This section is a bonus, but is important, especially if you would like to work again for the same teacher or school. Leave a note for the teacher you replace. Let them know how the class went, include who was absent, and mention if any students in particular were disruptive. It is a small gesture, but it means a lot to the teacher. It keeps them in the know of what happened in their classroom. You can write your note on a post-it or on the same piece of paper on which the teacher had written the instructions for you. Your note can follow a structure similar to the one on the following page:

Everybody worked well today. All students read chapters 8 and 9 and most finished the questions in class. I told those who have not finished to do so for homework. Jamie was a little disruptive, but she stayed on task for most of the period.

Absences: - Capelli, Lisa
- George, Bernard

It was a pleasure,

Julien Morizio

Place the note on the work you collected from the students (if any needed to be collected) and leave the documents on the desk if the teacher does not share the classroom with someone else. If that is not the case, then leave the documents either with the secretary or in the teacher's pigeonhole.

Extra:

The teacher might have missed their students. So, in your note, add a little something special that happened. It could be that the class wished Susan happy birthday, or that John did a very nice sketch, or that Mary finished quickly and helped a lot of her classmates – anything positive that helps the teacher place him/herself in the classroom that day and feel that they did not miss anything and that their students were in good hands. They will feel as though that substitute teacher cares as much as they do.

Doing Your Best

At the end of the day, there is only so much you can do. At once, you must adapt to a new environment, while at the same time handle around thirty youngsters. Remember that you are already doing the school, the teacher, and the students a great service by being there. If you take the job seriously, and build on what you learn through your experiences, you will do a better job every time. Hopefully this book has provided you with some information that will serve you well and help you as you get better at subbing.

If you retain anything from this book, hopefully it is to have the principles of structure, empathy, and fairness guide you as you work with the students you sub for. Keep in mind that they are just kids. You were a kid once. How did you feel when you had a substitute teacher? Which ones made a good impression on you? What did you think of those who yelled at the class and made fake threats? Please do not be like the substitute teachers you did not appreciate when you were younger. Instead, try to understand the students, be straightforward with them about what is expected of them, and always be fair.

References

Experience

Lubin, P. M. (2019, November 11). *Leadership Theory in Education* [Lecture notes]. McGill University.

Mendler, A. N. (2000). *Motivating Students Who Don't Care*. Bloomington, IN: Solution Tree Press.

Morizio, J. (2020). Choice and Motivation. *Responsive Tutoring*. https://www.responsivetutoring.com/post/choice-and-motivation

Greene, R. W. (2014). *The explosive child: a new approach for understanding and parenting easily frustrated, chronically inflexible children* (Revised and updated. Fifth). Harper.

www.ingramcontent.com/pod-product-compliance
Lightning Source LLC
Chambersburg PA
CBHW031920270726
48655CB00007BA/2843